Better Homes and Gardens®

HANDBOOK
OF
COMMON
MEDICINES

Frederic W. Platt, M.D., F.A.C.P.

Director of Internal Medicine
The Presbyterian Medical Center
Denver, Colorado

© 1980 by Meredith Corporation, Des Moines, Iowa.
All Rights Reserved. Printed in the United States of America.
First Edition. Third Printing, 1981.
Library of Congress Catalog Card Number: 80-66577
ISBN: 0-696-02043-2

DIALOGUE

Have you ever taken part in a patient-doctor dialogue such as this?:

DOCTOR:	PATIENT:

"Tell me now, are you taking any drugs?"

"Only the ones you prescribed for me, doctor."

"OK, exactly what drugs are you taking?"

"Well, there's the water pill, hykothorazide, and the heart medicine, dioxin, and the one for blood pressure—it's yellow."

"Do you take anything else?"

"Nope."

"Didn't we have you on something for gout?"

"Oh yeah, you mean the one starting with Z. I take that at night."

"Anything else for headache, or sleep, or bowels, or anything else?"

"Oh, I take a few Anacin but not all that many, and of course I use that natural herb laxative. Once in a while I take a Bufferin or Excedrin, but never any aspirin."

"Is that it then? No other pills or potions?"

"Well, that's it. Except for the B_{12} shots your nurse has been giving me and the pill the city health nurse gives me to clear up my X ray."

"B_{12} shots? Clear up your X ray?"

"Yeah, I went for an X ray and they told me I had a spot on it and it would probably be OK if I just took these pills for a year."

"OK, then that means you're taking hydrochlorothiazide, digoxin, probably Aldomet, Zyloprim, some over-the-counter pain medicines, some sort of laxative, B_{12} shots, and maybe an anti-TB drug. Is that all?"

"You got it, doc. I'm no drug addict, you know."

This sort of dialogue is fairly common. Most people do not realize how many potentially toxic drugs they use (medicines are drugs), they forget the names of drugs they take, and they give no thought at all to the significance of pills bought without a prescription—despite the fact that an enormous number of effective and dangerous medicines are readily available. Many over-the-counter pills are potentially as hazardous as prescription items, and products that combine several agents introduce complex and confusing drug interactions.

People over 40 are not necessarily more susceptible to drug reactions than younger people, but as we grow older, chronic conditions requiring programs of medication are likely to surface, introducing new drugs to interact with "self treatment" items that one may take habitually or sporadically. It is well to know that no effective drug is totally harmless to all people in all doses at all times, and you should tell your doctor about everything you are taking for presumed health reasons—even vitamins, some of which can be toxic in large doses. As much as 10 percent of national medical costs (now about $200 billion annually in the United States) goes for the care of adverse drug reactions.

What you should know. With respect to any form of treatment, the consumer should at least be informed of the nature of the disease or disorder being treated, what the proposed treatment is intended to accomplish, and what "bad" or side effects of that treatment might possibly happen, along with the good. Most states have laws regarding informed consent that make these requirements clear. When several prescribed drugs are used together, complexities increase geometrically, and the total hazards of interaction may be unknown. Complexity is further increased if common over-the-counter drugs are combined with other medications.

ADVERSE DRUG EFFECTS

Undesired drug effects are produced by different mechanisms. There are many ways to get a bad result with a drug. The problem may be inherent in the nature of the drug, or may accompany a desired action. Or, it may be due to misuse, or the idiosyncrasies of a particular patient.

Simple overdose is the most common cause of bad reactions. One ends up with too much of a desired result—sometimes from the mistaken belief that "if a little is good, a lot is better." For example, if a diuretic drug is used to rid the body of excess salts and fluid, it may do this to such excess that the result is dehydration and dangerous loss of dissolved minerals (electrolytes).

Another example is that of anticoagulants or "blood thinners" that are used to prevent abnormal clotting of the blood in arteries, veins, or chambers of the heart. Too much anticoagulation interferes with the protective clotting mechanism so that hemorrhage may result.

Antibiotics are used to kill off disease-causing bacteria. However, too large a dose may destroy friendly bacteria in the gastrointestinal tract with which we live comfortably and normally. This may leave the way clear for fungi and bacteria that cause disease to proliferate in the gut and cause serious trouble.

Overdosage is not always the patient's fault. For many reasons, determination of a correct dose is no easy matter. People vary in their personal chemistry, age, weight, hypersensitivities, and other factors affecting drug actions. With some drugs—digitalis, for example—the toxic dose is close to the therapeutic dose, so that initial calculations must be carefully made and perhaps adjusted to the patient's response. And because internal conditions of the body change, an initially correct dose of a drug taken for a long time may be too large later on. One should be aware of possible side effects of a drug so that if any occur, the physician can be alerted. It is often possible to lessen undesired effects by adjusting the dose slightly.

Secondary effects. These are the second most common type of adverse drug reactions. They occur because a drug has some effect or effects other than that for which it is primarily given. For example, *antihistamine* drugs block allergic reactions, but some of them have a significant secondary action: sedation. They can make one feel drowsy and dull and make it hazardous to drive a car, run a punch press, cross a busy street, or do anything else that demands alertness and coordination.

As another example, *phenothiazine* drugs are very effective tranquilizers and anti-nausea medications. But sometimes they produce bizarre posture and movement disorders, with writhing or twisting of the body. Still another: *diuretics* cause an elevated blood uric acid level and can precipitate an attack of gout in a susceptible person.

Allergy, a third mechanism, is familiar to most people, but actually is less common than overdosage or secondary effects. Perhaps the most common drug allergy is reaction to *penicillin,* an old and excellent antibiotic that, if administered in the past, can alter the body's immune-defense system so that a subsequent injection may produce a relatively minor skin rash, an asthma-like constriction of the breathing passages, and even swelling of the larynx resulting in fatal suffocation.

Physicians customarily ask a new patient if he or she is sensitive to penicillin (or other drugs), but in an emergency, an unconscious person cannot answer. People who know that they are sensitive to penicillin (or other medications) should carry a statement to that effect in their billfolds, or wear a special identification tag or bracelet so stating.

Different drugs seem to have specific capacities for producing different sorts of allergic responses. Most side effects of this nature are a matter of a bad combination of patient and drug.

Multiple drugs constitute a major fourth category of adverse drug effects. These drug + drug + patient combinations are very complicated and less predictable than "simple" overdose, secondary, or allergic reactions.

For instance, a patient who takes *Coumadin,* an anticoagulant drug, and later develops an attack of gouty arthritis (in no way related to the Coumadin), might be treated with *phenylbutazone* (Butazolidin). This drug is usually excellent for treating gout. However, phenylbutazone will displace Coumadin from blood proteins, leading to a higher level of free Coumadin, a higher degree of anticoagulation, and eventually excessive bleeding.

The dangers of combining beverage alcohol with sedatives (tranquilizers, sleeping pills, and relaxants) are fairly well known. Technically, these drugs are *depressants* (alcohol is a drug). A person who can tolerate an accustomed amount of alcohol perfectly well, and a familiar dose of a sedative equally well, may, if the two drugs are consumed at more or less the same time, be plunged into deep coma and even death.

Finally, mistakes occur. Patients drink toxic Phisohex soap instead of bathing with it. Illegible prescriptions may be misinterpreted by a pharmacist. Patients lose bottle labels, they don't read them, or they don't understand them.

The adverse drug effects we've mentioned are common and dangerous. But an even more common drug problem is failure of a drug to do any good because the patient doesn't take it or doesn't follow directions. This is not drug failure but patient failure, and many things contribute to it. The drug may be costly, so the prescription goes unfilled. Or the doctor's instructions may be unclear or unemphasized. And, some people resist taking any medicine at all.

A drug may be so beneficial that minor side effects are no great deterrent, considering the good accomplished. A well-advised patient will know what medications he is taking, will ask about adverse effects to be aware of, and will minimize the use of drugs of all sorts.

WHAT IS A DRUG?

Definition of a drug seems easy: a foreign substance given by a doctor to a patient to alleviate disease or improve health. However, drugs need not be foreign to the body, they often are not recommended by a physician, and they may seem to have little to do with health or disease.

Drugs may be normal substances of the body, such as potassium salts or thyroid hormone. They may be foodstuffs, such as milk or vitamins. The word "drug" takes on an evil meaning when associated with "drug addicts" and "dope pushers" who illicitly use and sell narcotics, cocaine, "uppers" and "downers" (stimulants and sedatives), and mind-altering agents. However, even these are important medicines when they are prescribed for a patient by a doctor.

Confusion of names

People are wisely told to "read the label," not only of drug packages but of household cleansers, foods, paints, and everyday items that list ingredients and tell how to use the product. Hundreds of drugs are sold without prescription and are considered to be safe when *used as directed.* But it's quite possible to take toxic overdoses of commonplace household medicines if warnings are not heeded. We recognize brand names, but the technical names of specific drugs are too arcane to be informative to the ordinary purchaser.

Every recognized drug has a chemical name, a generic name, and usually a brand or trade name that the manufacturer hopes you will remember. The chemical name, which describes the structure of the drug molecule, is the most informative of all, but unfortunately it can only be understood by a graduate chemist or a dabbler in nomenclature. The generic name is a little simpler, but still has an esoteric sound of chemistry. For example:

Chemical name	6-chloro-3,4-dihydro-7-sulfamyl-2H-1,2,4-benzothiadiazine-1,1-dioxide
Generic name	hydrochlorothiazide
Trade name	Esidrix, Hydrodiuril, Oretic, and others

Any manufacturer with the capability can produce hydrochlorothiazide. But he cannot market it under another manufacturer's brand name, and will have to devise his own or sell the drug under its generic name with the manufacturer identified.

Prescribing by generic name is often advocated on the premise that the cost to the patient should be less. With only a few exceptions, there is little evidence that a brand-name drug is superior to the same

Frequently prescribed drugs

Trade name	Generic name	Trade name	Generic name
Achromycin	tetracycline	Darvon	propoxyphene
Aerosporin	polymyxin B	Decadron	dexamethasone
Albamycin	novobiocin	Declomycin	demeclocycline
Aldactone	spironolactone	Delalutin	hydroxyproges-terone caproate
Aldomet	alphamethyldopa		
Amytal	amobarbital	Delta-Cortef	prednisolone
Antabuse	disulfiram	Deltasone	prednisone
Antivert	meclizine	Demerol	meperidine
Anturane	sulfinpyrazone	Depo-medrol	methyl predniso-lone acetate
Apresoline	hydralazine		
Aralen	chloroquine	Dexedrine	dextroampheta-mine sulfate
Aristocort	triamcinolone		
Artane	trihexyphenidyl	Diabinese	chlorpropamide
Aspirin (originally, but no longer, a trade name)	acetylsalicylic acid	Diamox	acetazolamide
		Dianabol	methandrosteno-lone
Atarax	hydroxyzine	Dilantin	diphenylhydantoin
Atromid-S	clofibrate	Diuril	chlorothiazide
Aureomycin	chlortetracycline	Doriden	glutethimide
		Dramamine	dimenhydrinate
Bactocill	oxacillin	Durabolin	nandrolone phen-propionate
Benadryl	diphenhydramine		
Benemid	probenecid	Dymelor	acetohexamide
Benzedrine	amphetamine sulfate	Dynapen	dicloxacillin
		Dyrenium	triamterene
Bicillin	benzathine penicillin	Elavil	amitriptyline hydrochloride
Brethine	terbutaline		
Butazolidin	phenylbutazone	Enduron	methyclothiazide
		Erythrocin	erythromycin
Cardilate	erythrityl tetrani-trate	Equanil	meprobamate
		Esidrix	hydrochlorothia-zide
Catapres	clonidine		
Cedanilid	lanantoside C	Eskabarb	phenobarbital
Celestone	betamethasone		
Chloromycetin	chloramphenicol	Flagyl	metronidazole
Chlor-Trimeton	chlorpheniramine maleate	Florinef Acetate	fluorocortisone acetate
Cleocin	clindamycin	Fulvicin	griseofulvin
Colace	dioctyl sodium sul-fosuccinate	Fungizone	amphotericin B
		Furacin	nitrofurazone
Colymycin	colistin	Furadantin	nitrofurantoin
Compazine	prochlorperazine		
Cortef	hydrocortisone	Gantanol	sulfamethoxazole
Coumadin	warfarin	Gantrisin	sulfisoxazole
Cytomel	triiodothyronine or T 3	Garamycin	gentamycin
		Geopin	carbenicillin
		Gitaligin	gitalin
Dalmane	flurazepam hydro-chloride	Grifulvin	griseofulvin
		Griasctin	griseofulvin

Trade name	Generic name	Trade name	Generic name
Haldol	haloperidol	Miltown	meprobamate
Haldrone	paramethasone acetate	Minipress	prazosin
		Moderil	rescinnamine
Halotestin	fluoxymesterone	Motrin	ibuprofen
Harmonyl	deserpidine	Mucomyst	acetylcysteine
Hexadrol	dexamethasone	Myambutol	ethambutol hydrochloride
Hydeltrasol	prednisolone		
Hydrodiuril	hydrochlorothiazide	Mycostatin	nystatin
		Myleran	busulfan
Hyperstat	diazoxide	Myochrysine	gold sodium thiomalate
Hygroton	chlorthalidone		
Ilosone	erythromycin estolate	Nalline	nalorphine
		Naprosyn	naproxen
Ilotycin	erythromycin	Nardil	phenelzine sulfate
Imuran	azathioprine	Nembutal	pentobarbital
Inderal	propranolol	Neo-Synephrine	phenylephrine
Indocin	indomethacin	Nilevar	norethandrolone
Ismelin	guanethidine sulfate	Noctec	chloral hydrate
		Noludar	methyprylon
Isordil	isosorbide dinitrate	Norpace	disopyramide
Isuprel	isoproterenol	Norpramin	desipramine hydrochloride
Kafocin	cephaloglycin	Omnipen	ampicillin
Kantrex	kanamycin	Oncovin	vincristine sulfate
Keflex	cephalexin	Oretic	hydrochlorothiazide
Keflin	cephalothin		
Kenalog	triamcinolone	Oreton	testosterone propionate
Lanoxin	digoxin	Orinase	tolbutamide
Larodopa	levodopa		
Lasix	furosemide	Panmycin	tetracycline
Leukeran	chlorambucil	Panwarfin	warfarin
Librium	chlordiazepoxide	Parnate	tranylcypromine
Lincocin	lincomycin	Pathocil	dicloxacillin
Lithane	lithium carbonate	Penbritin	ampicillin
Lopressor	metoprolol	Pentothal	thiopental
Luminal	phenobarbital	Pen Vee K	potassium phenoxymethyl penicillin
Mandelamine	methenamine mandelate	Peritrate	pentaerythritol tetranitrate
Marezine	cyclizine	Persantine	dipyridamole
Mellaril	thioridazine	Phenergan	promethazine
Mephyton	phytonadione	Phenurone	phenacemide
Mesantoin	mephenytoin	Placidyl	ethchlorvynol
Mestinon	pyridostigmine	Plaquenil	hydroxychloroquine
Meticortelone	prednisolone		
Meticorten	prednisone	Polycillin	ampicillin
Midicel	sulfamethoxypyridazine	Premarin	conjugated estrogens

Frequently prescribed drugs

Trade name	Generic name	Trade name	Generic name
Pro-Banthine	propantheline bromide	Temaril	trimeprazine tartrate
Pronestyl	procainamide	Tempra	acetaminophen
Prostaphlin	oxacillin	Tensilon	edrophonium chloride
Prostigmin	neostigmine bromide	Terramycin	oxytetracycline
Purinethol	6-mercaptopurine	Tetracyn	tetracycline
Pyopen	carbenicillin	Tetrex	tetracycline
Pyribenzamine	tripelennamine	Thiomerin	mercaptomerin
		Thorazine	chlorpromazine
Questran	cholestyramine	Thyrolar	liotrix
Quinaglute	quinidine gluconate	Tinactin	tolnaftate
Quinidex	quinidine sulfate	Tindal	acetophenazine maleate
Rau-Sed	reserpine	Tofranil	imipramine hydrochloride
Regitine	phentolamine		
Ritalin	methylphenidate	Tolinase	tolazamide
Robitussin	guaifenesin	Trilafon	perphenazine
Rondomycin	methacycline	Tylenol	acetaminophen
Saluron	hydroflumethiazide	Urecholine	bethanechol chloride
Seconal	secobarbital	Unipen	sodium nafcillin
Serax	oxazepam	Ulticillin VK	potassium phenoxymethyl penicillin
Serpasil	reserpine		
Sinequan	doxepin		
Solganal	aurothioglucose	Valisone	betamethasone
Solu-Cortef	hydrocortisone sodium succinate	Valium	diazepam
		Valmid	ethinamate
Soxomide	sulfisoxazole	Vanceril	beclomethasone
Sparine	promazine hydrochloride	Vancocin	vancomycin
		Vasoxyl	methoxamine hydrochloride
Staphcillin	methicillin		
Stelazine	trifluoperazine	V-Cillin K	potassium phenoxymethyl penicillin
Sulfathalidine	phthalylsulfathiazole		
Sumycin	tetracycline	Velban	vinblastine sulfate
Synalar	fluocinolone acetonide	Veracillin	dicloxacillin
		Versapen	hetacillin
Synthroid	levothyroxine or T4	Vibramycin	doxycycline
		Vioform	iodochlorhydroxyquin
TACE	chlorotrianisene		
Tacaryl	methdilazine	Vistaril	hydroxyzine pamoate
Tagamet	cimetidine		
Talwin	pentazocine hydrochloride	Winstrol	stanozolol
		Wycillin	procaine penicillin G
Tandearil	oxyphenbutazone		
Taractan	chlorprothixene		
TAO	triacetyloleandomycin	Zarontin	ethosuximide
Tapazole	methimazole	Zyloprim	allopurinol

drug under its generic name produced by another manufacturer. However, the cost of a prescription seems to vary more from pharmacy to pharmacy than from trade name to trade name. It is customary to identify a drug, either by its trade or generic name, on the prescription label. In describing a drug, the generic name is usually written first, followed by the trade name in parentheses.

The preceding list, by no means complete, gives the trade and generic names of frequently prescribed single drugs (not combinations). We shall later have some general comment on their therapeutic actions.

Formidable as this list appears to be, it is a small fraction of medications available under various names. A standard reference work, the *Physicians' Desk Reference,* lists upward of 8,000 brand names, and new ones are continually added.

Drug interactions are increasingly important when taking more than one drug at a time. Drugs today are more powerful than they were in the past. Interactions may occur not only between potent drugs, but also between potent and seemingly innocuous ones. For instance, many antacids are sold over the counter to combat excess stomach acid and reduce symptoms of heartburn or indigestion. If a person takes tetracycline, a widely prescribed antibiotic, and takes such an antacid at the same time, the antacid will reduce the effectiveness of the antibiotic by preventing absorption of tetracycline in the body. The wisdom of telling your doctor about every medication you are taking should be obvious.

Dosage

The size of a drug tablet is no gauge of its potency. The basic unit of dosage is 1 gram, about 1/28th of an ounce. Most drug dosages are prescribed in milligrams (one-thousandth of a gram), written mg. A common dosage of digoxin, a digitalis preparation, is ¼ milligram (0.25 mg) — so minuscule an amount that it is invisible to the naked eye. Thus, it is buried in a tablet made of inert material that probably weighs 100 mg, or 400 times the weight of the active drug.

Diazepam (Valium), a frequently prescribed tranquilizer, is given in 5-mg doses. This, too, must be buried in a larger carrier tablet. Aspirin is given in 325-mg dosage, and so needs no carrier other than something to hold the drug powder together. An older apothecary system uses *grains* instead of grams as a weight index. One grain weighs about 65 mg.

Combination drugs

A great many drugs, sold or dispensed under single brand names, are combinations of two or more active agents. The great majority of over-the-counter drugs, except plain aspirin, contain two or three ingredients, and some as many as seven or eight. The rationale is sometimes questionable, as in a product containing drugs that loosen the sputum and make coughing easier and more productive, along with ingredients that suppress coughing.

Many medicines prescribed by doctors combine different drugs in a single tablet or capsule for practical and therapeutic reasons. These often cost less than the constituents taken separately and the patient is more likely to take his medicine with regularity. Many studies have shown that patients skip, forget, or miss more of their medications when numerous drugs are prescribed than when only a few are given, and the most common reason why drugs don't help patients is failure to take them as directed. This is no trivial problem.

There are some disadvantages to combining medications, too. A combination provides a fixed ratio of constituents where a greater proportion of one or another may be more desirable. Patient and doctor may forget the ingredients and begin to think of the combination as a single drug, so if interactions occur or some laboratory test is mysteriously inaccurate, it may be difficult to identify an offending ingredient.

Are drugs really health potions?

Physicians view drugs as specific remedies. A drug is prescribed *for* something — either a specific treatment for a diagnosed disorder, or at least a medicine with specific action to alleviate a bothersome symptom.

Some people assume that drugs have limitless powers for good, which is not the case. They seem to act as if a drug is "good for what ails you," and even healthy persons may have great expectations from "tonics," nostrums, and exotic "natural" substances that assertedly can make us feel better than we do. A multimillion-dollar business in over-the-counter products thrives on very human yearnings to bubble with energy, look like a sylph, banish that tired feeling, and be the life of the party, merely by swallowing magic. Some vendors use pseudo-medical people in advertisements to give a false impression of medical authority. When you hear that "four out of five doctors recommend . . .," do you wonder about the fifth?

Prescription drugs also can be misused in ways the prescriber never intended. A drug is prescribed for you and you alone, in specific dosage, for a diagnosed condition. Many people hoard leftover pills from past illnesses—some of them have miniature pharmacies in cabinet drawers—and hand out drugs to relatives and friends whose complaints seem to warrant it. The intent is good, but the uninformed dispenser of pharmaceutical goodwill is unlikely to know much about interactions and contraindications that physicians are aware of.

What can an intelligent person do? Avoid any medications unless they are deemed necessary by a well-trained diagnostician. Then take the prescription as prescribed. If a ten-day course is prescribed, take the medicine for ten days (even if you feel better after five days). Immediately report any unexpected effect to your physician. Avoid over-the-counter remedies as best you can. And assume that all drugs are potentially poisonous. They are.

Is there such a thing as a health tonic? Perhaps. Fresh air, exercise, meaningful work, friendship, love, and a sense of fulfillment are great tonics. But none of these has yet been put into a package by the pharmaceutical industry.

COMMONLY PRESCRIBED DRUGS AND THEIR ACTIONS

The rest of this chapter gives brief descriptions of commonly used drugs, their applications, and possible side effects or hazards. The drugs are grouped according to therapeutic actions. In most instances, they are identified by generic names, which can be equated with brand names by scanning the list previously given. In no case is the discussion complete. There are many other groups of medications that are not mentioned.

Sedatives

These drugs have been available longer than most current medications. In popular language, they are "sleeping pills," inducing drowsiness and sleep. In doing so, they diminish excitement, anxiety, and physical activity. Their most common adverse effect is over-sedation—unwanted sleepiness or too deep a sleep, stupor, or even coma. Sedatives in very large doses are often taken in suicide attempts that are frequently successful. Various drugs in this group, not so difficult to come by as "hard" drugs such as heroin, may be grossly abused by young people who take them in large doses for kicks (the street-slang name is "downers").

Barbiturates. Most drugs in this group, derived from barbituric acid, can be recognized by names that end in "-al"; for example, *phenobarbital, secobarbital,* and *pentobarbital.* They are cheap and effective sleep-inducers for short-term use, although the sleep induced is not exactly natural since the restful dreaming phase of sleep is obliterated. Chronic or long-term use is another matter. Dependency and even true physiologic addiction can occur in a relatively short time. There is no specific antidote for barbiturate poisoning. Treatment of barbiturate addiction is very difficult, and withdrawal symptoms are more severe and serious than those of morphine or heroin withdrawal.

The use of barbiturates adds difficulty to the use of other drugs that are transformed in the liver. Interference by barbiturates is a serious problem in anticoagulant *(warfarin)* therapy.

Non-barbiturates. Other sleep-promoting *(hypnotic)* drugs of different chemical structure are loosely grouped as non-barbiturate sedatives. The more potent ones (such as chloral hydrate and glutethimide) are sold on prescription. Some antihistamine drugs, such as methapyrilene, have sedative properties and are components of numerous sleep products sold over the counter, in dosages low enough to be considered safe when used as directed. However, excessive amounts of antihistamines can lead to an agitated, frightened,

hallucinating state known as organic delirium, and may produce coma.

Insomnia, or what a person construes to be insomnia, is the main reason for resort to sleeping aids. Sleep is desirable, indeed inevitable, but wakefulness for two or three days has little harmful effect. Lack of one or two nights' sleep is not debilitating; it's worrying about not having slept that does most of the harm.

If one's sleep is actually less than the body's physiologic requirements—true insomnia—there may be organic causes that should be discovered and treated. But a vast amount of distress arises from erroneous beliefs about sleep, for instance, that one must sleep at least eight hours a night for health and physical and mental vigor. This is a fair average but far from a universal yardstick. Not counting naps or daytime dozing, aging people may require, or think they require, more night-time sleep than they get. As we grow older there is a reduction in the deep-sleep stages of slumber, so that a feeling of having slept profoundly is diminished. All of this can lead to chronic use and dependence on sleeping pills to attain the supposedly ideal eight hours of sleep that may well be excessive for many older people.

Tranquilizers

In recent years, a number of drugs have been developed that calm the patient but don't put him or her to sleep. These are popularly called "tranquilizers." None is entirely free of sedative properties, and an overdose still may cause coma. As a group, these drugs are commonly classified as "major" and "minor" tranquilizers.

"Major" tranquilizers. A major group of tranquilizers is the *phenothiazines.* The

prototype is *chlorpromazine,* and many drugs in this group can be recognized by generic names that end in "-azine" *(trifluoperazine, promazine, thioridazine,* and *prochlorperazine).*

Selection of the right drug requires medical discrimination, for although different phenothiazines have many similarities, there are significant differences in their potencies and actions. Their initial successes in enabling many patients in mental hospitals to return to society has labeled them as drugs for psychosis or severe mental illness. Indeed, they have largely superseded the use of electroshock therapy in mental hospitals, but they have many other applications as well.

Certain phenothiazines decrease nausea and vomiting, and are widely used for that purpose. The drugs have a calming effect on extreme agitation and anxiety, and increase the effectiveness of sedatives.

However, this group of drugs is plagued with annoying and rather unpredictable muscular side effects called movement disorders. These range from trivial tic-like lip-smacking to writhing or jerking movements of the entire body. These movement disorders usually cease when the offending drug is discontinued, but may become permanent if the drug is continued for months after the movement disorders appear. Another problem associated with the drugs is a drop in the patient's blood pressure. This could be beneficial to a person with high blood pressure, but dangerous to one with normal pressure.

"Minor" tranquilizers. These drugs help to ameliorate less-severe anxiety, tension, and psychosomatic symptoms, as well as emotional "wrought-upness" resulting from stresses in the environment. They are similar to barbiturates in many ways, but are less likely to induce sleep or drowsiness or impair performance. Representative drugs in this group are *chlordiazepoxide, diazepam, haloperidol, meprobamate,* and *hydroxyzine.*

The minor tranquilizers in proper doses for anxiety and tension are usually well tolerated, but chronic use may produce dependence on the drugs. Possible side effects are headaches, increased urinary frequency, fainting, and reduced tolerance to other drugs.

Another tranquilizer, major in its effects on individuals and society, is ethyl alcohol, the drinking kind. It is addictive to about 10 percent of its users, and leads to grave diseases of the brain, stomach, liver, heart, and pancreas. Tranquilizers and sedatives, like alcohol, are depressants of the central nervous system, and combined use is dangerous and sometimes fatal.

The enormous amount of tranquilizers dispensed in the United States suggests that we are an anxiety-ridden culture, or that we naively seek "a pill for every problem." Many reviews of the tranquilizer market suggest that we are fortunate that the drugs do not do more harm than they do, and that their use is often a retreat from a real attempt to understand and solve problems. Some tension is necessary to deal with the challenges of everyday living, and total tranquillity is total torpidity.

Antidepressants and stimulants

Depression—not ordinary "blues" that pass away, but profound, Stygian, everlasting gloom—is a tremendous and not uncommon burden that saps physical and mental energies and can lead to contemplation of suicide. Many drugs to lift the spirits have been tried and found wanting. Now we have available some true antidepressants that can lighten the burden of despair borne by severely depressed people. However, these drugs are not panaceas. In excess dosages, they may lead to irregularities of the heartbeat, confusion, coma, and high or low swings in blood pressure. There are numerous possible interactions with other drugs and even foods.

MAO inhibitors. A major family of antidepressants is called MAO inhibitors because they inhibit an enzyme, for which the initials suffice. Generic names of some of these drugs are *tranylcypromine* and *phenelzine.*

There are many relatively minor adverse reactions to the drugs, but the most serious is a sudden and extreme rise in blood pressure, from interactions with other drugs or foodstuffs. Peculiarly, dangerously high blood pressure can be provoked by eating aged cheese, beer, wine, pickled herring, and chicken liver. Interactions with other drugs are so numerous and mysterious that it is important to know what other medicines are being taken.

For example, MAO drugs can potentiate or intensify the actions of certain antihypertensive drugs, causing a drop in blood pressure. Also, they can potentiate insulin, causing low blood sugar (insulin shock), as well as barbiturates and anesthetics. Stimulating drugs known as *sympathomimetics* (see *Amphetamines*) can interact with MAO inhibitors to produce severe headache, high blood pressure, and heart irregularities. Such stimulants may be taken inadvertently; some over-the-counter cold remedies contain them.

Tricyclics. Other major antidepressants are classed as *tricyclics,* from their chemical structure. The prototypes are *imipramine* and *amitryptyline,* and they are the most widely prescribed antidepressants. They are shorter acting than MAO inhibitors, more rapid in their onset of action, and do not potentiate other commonly prescribed drugs. However, possible adverse effects are numerous, and the drugs are contraindicated for patients with severe heart disease or glaucoma.

Amphetamines. These minor stimulants, in popular language, are "pep pills." In the argot of drug abusers who take large doses to get "high," they are "uppers," "Bennies," "Red Jackets," and other names referring to the color of the capsules. Another area of their abuse is the use of such drugs to keep awake for unconscionably long periods of time, ending in collapse when the fatigue debt must be repaid.

The drugs act upon the sympathetic nervous system and hence are called sympathomimetic (imitating) agents. As a group, they are called *amphetamines,* from the parent drug; other forms are *dextroamphetamine, methamphetamine,* and *methylphenidate.*

For many years, amphetamines were prescribed in normal dosages to reduce depression and to try to decrease appetite of reducers. At one time, more than 90 companies marketed such products. However, their use has declined since the Food and Drug Administration determined that they are of little effectiveness in either depression or obesity. Moreover, their misuse can lead to addiction, overstimulation, jerky reflexes, agitation, and deleterious effects on the heart.

Antibiotics

Now and then a patient says, "Doc, I need a shot of penicillin for my cold." There is touching faith that antibiotics are entirely harmless drugs and that they can cure any infection. Neither is the case. This is not to imply that antibiotics are not tremendously valuable—only that today there are dozens of antibiotics, quite different in their actions and adverse effects and the or-

"All drugs are potentially dangerous, whether sold by prescription or over the counter."

ganisms they attack, so that selection of the right drug and dosage requires no little medical know-how. Next to tranquilizers, antibiotics are the most frequently prescribed drugs in the United States.

How antibiotics work. Some antibiotics destroy bacteria by disrupting the germ's cell walls. Others, slower in action, interfere with protein synthesis so the bacterium has no hope of posterity. This gives time for the patient's own defenses to subdue the infection. Other complex germ-and-drug interactions are not well-understood.

Agents to combat disease-causing bacteria, fungi, protozoans, and larger organisms are now available. The great exceptions are viruses. Only a rare viral disease such as trachoma or psittacosis responds to antibiotics. The common cold and the many viruses that cause influenza-like diseases are totally unaffected by antibiotics.

Varieties of antibiotics. The first antibiotics were derived from molds and fungi, memorialized in terms such as "-mycin" and "-cillin" in many of their names. Notably, a moldy cantaloupe from a produce market in Peoria furnished a high-yielding strain for producing penicillin, which ushered in the antibiotic age. Antibiotics are far more numerous than drugs in most other categories; indeed, they have proliferated enormously.

Today, many antibiotics are semi-synthetic — the products of chemical modification of their molecules designed to make them effective against specific organisms, to broaden their spectrum of action, to lessen side effects, or to offer a choice when patients are sensitive to an antibiotic or when microbes are resistant to it. Some of this proliferation is redundant, but much of it has led to very useful variations. Synthetic modifications of the penicillin group have been very fruitful, yielding antibiotics that are effective against resistant bacteria, which produce an enzyme that destroys the basic penicillin molecule.

Adverse effects of antibiotics are plentiful. Their very destruction of bacteria can paradoxically cause the multiplication of resistant and dangerous bacteria by decreasing the competition for nutrients. "Superinfection" resulting from such therapy has led to hospital-wide epidemics.

In addition, many antibiotics have direct toxic effects on the kidney, the nerves of hearing, the gastrointestinal tract, or the bone marrow. Others have frequently triggered allergic reactions that are worse than the disorder being treated. For instance, sporadic doses of penicillin over periods of time can set the stage for hypersensitivity reactions ranging from a mild skin rash to suffocation from congestion of the larynx.

Surprisingly, some of the more toxic antibiotics have turned out to be effective anti-cancer drugs. Their hazards are recognized, but treatment is justified by the seriousness of the underlying disease.

Sulfas. Drugs known as *sulfonamides* were the first "magic bullets"—agents that directly attacked specific organisms in the bloodstream without doing significant harm to the patient. They preceded antibiotics by a decade, and inaugurated a pharmaceutical revolution that has benefited two generations of patients. The sulfas are relatively simple, inexpensive compounds whose generic names carry the prefix "sulfa-."

Innumerable sulfas have been created by chemists, and the drugs are important antimicrobial agents. They are still used in treating urinary tract and a few uncommon infections, and for special purposes such as preparing the bowel for surgery. Toxic reactions to the newer sulfas are quite rare, but they do occur and the patient should be alert to any untoward symptoms.

A large group of antibiotics, the aminoglycosides, are available only by injection and are given intramuscularly and intravenously. No orally absorbable form of this group has been found.

Digitalis

Before the twentieth century, only a few drugs with specific actions were available to physicians—digitalis, quinine, and a few vaccines and antitoxins. It is hard to say which is more striking, the centuries of plagues and diseases for which physicians had almost no effective medicines, or the great numbers of potent and effective drugs that have been developed in the past half century.

Digitalis is a drug with a venerable history and is one likely to become familiar, at least by name, to many persons who develop some form of heart trouble as the years roll on. William Withering, a British physician, brought digitalis into medical use in the latter part of the eighteenth century. He began to treat patients who had "the dropsy" or edema—puffy, boggy accumulations of fluid in tissues—with extracts of the foxglove plant *(digitalis purpurea)*. He noted that the foxglove caused patients to pass great amounts of urine and to lose the edema.

Withering thought that the drug must act on the patient's kidneys. Now it is known that digitalis acts mainly on the heart, causing it to contract more forcefully and pump a greater volume of blood with each beat. The strengthened contractions supply more blood to all vital organs, including the kidneys, and it is to this greater blood flow that the decrease of edema can be credited.

Digitalis also causes a blockage in electrical transmission from the upper to the lower chambers of the heart. In conditions where the upper chambers beat too rapidly, the drug allows the important hard-pumping lower chambers to slow and strengthen.

Standard preparations include powdered foxglove leaf, but purified fractions of the active agent are most commonly prescribed. These include *digoxin, digitoxin, gitalin,* and *lanatoside.* Probably 80 percent of patients on digitalis take digoxin.

This drug has captured a large share of the digitalis market since a widely available test of the blood digoxin level has been developed. Being able to monitor the drug level has helped avoid some of the toxic side effects of the drug.

Adverse effects. Even with the available tests of blood levels, there are no perfect tests for adjusting digitalis dosage, so the physician must rely on his judgment of the patient's condition. This is particularly true when the drug is first begun (initial digitalization), but digitalis is ordinarily taken over long periods of time or a lifetime, and possible toxic effects must be continually watched for. Relatively mild reactions include decreased appetite, nausea, and malaise. More serious toxic effect is irregularity of the heartbeat. Life-threatening arrhythmias can occur and are the major hazard of the drug.

Antiarrhythmic drugs
(Heartbeat Stabilizers)

The normal heart beats regularly and steadily at a rate that is usually between 60 and 100 beats per minute at rest, but faster with exercise. Various causes may throw this regular rhythm seriously, frighteningly, or just harmlessly out of kilter.

Drugs that act in various ways can be helpful in arrhythmic disorders. They may suppress an irritable focus of the heart's own pacemaker or they may impede electrical transmission down the line. The most frequently used antiarrhythmic agents are:

Drug	Common Adverse Effect
Propranolol	Wheezing, heart pump failure
Procainamide	Joint pain, arthritis
Quinidine	Platelet depression and bleeding
Digitalis	Further arrhythmias, nausea and vomiting

Digitalis, as mentioned, is given about as often for its antiarrhythmic action as for strengthening the heart muscle. Yet a complication of digitalis use may be an arrhythmia. When a patient develops such a complication, it may be very difficult to decide whether to give more or less digitalis.

Antihypertensives

Medically, the term hypertension means not emotional stress but abnormally high blood pressure. It is a common, often "silent" disorder, usually of undeterminable cause. The mainstays of current treatment are drugs.

A large number of diverse drugs are effective in lowering elevated blood pressure. In most instances, their precise mechanism of action is unclear. Many patients require a trial of one or another drug, or a combination of several drugs that add to each others' effects, until the most acceptable and effective dosage is determined. In general, in treating hypertension, one drug is chosen and its dosage is increased until a satisfactory level of pressure is maintained, or a limiting dosage is reached, in which case a second and perhaps a third drug will be added. Besides diuretics, described opposite, drugs of differing action and with a proliferation of brand names are useful in controlling hypertension.

Autonomic nervous system drugs such as *methyl dopa, reserpine, guanethidine,* and others interfere with nerve signals to muscles that constrict blood vessels. The general effect is to keep vessels more dilated so less pressure is needed to move blood through them. As with all antihypertensive agents, the most common adverse effect is a striking drop in blood pressure, even to the point of fainting, usually when the patient stands up.

Other adverse reactions include anemia, liver damage, emotional depression, and impotence.

Initally, *propranolol* was used to combat augmented heart activity when *hydralazine,* a vessel dilator, was used. It now seems that propanolol may be very effective even in the absence of such drugs. Hydralazine occasionally leads to a syndrome that resembles the rare disease systemic lupus erythematosus, with joint pains. This syndrome also has appeared after use of the antiarrhythmic *procainamide* and other drugs.

A number of newer drugs have appeared on the market in the last three years, all initially showing great promise in the treatment of high blood pressure. As each has been used more, however, problems have appeared. So far, there is no easy treatment of this most common and hazardous condition.

Diuretics

These drugs cause the kidneys to increase their production of urine and therefore the body's loss of salt and water. Commonly used diuretics are numerous members of the *thiazide* family, including *hydrochlorothiazide,* as well as *furosamide, triampterene,* and *aldactone.*

Diuretics are useful in conditions of a different nature that cause tissues to hold puffy accumulations of fluid. This edema may result from congestive heart failure, where the heart no longer pumps an adequate volume of blood; from cirrhosis of the liver, a disease in which excess fluid is retained; and from nephrosis, a kidney disease in which much protein is lost in the urine, paradoxically leading to fluid accumulation.

Along with loss of excess fluid, which is desired, diuretics can cause loss of dissolved minerals (electrolytes) that are important to the body. Especially, they can lead to derangements of blood sodium or potassium levels. The potassium level bears careful observation and is usually checked every few months in patients who take diuretics over the long term. Some patients may require potassium supplements prescribed by their physician; others may maintain normal potassium levels simply by eating potassium-rich foods.

Diuretics are also useful in treating hypertension, and are often used for less serious and transient problems of fluid accumulation, but if possible, they should be avoided in minor conditions because of their hazards.

Analgesics

Relief of pain has been a goal of pharmacology since antiquity. If pain is controllable, one can bear almost any other disability.

The most effective pain-relieving drugs are related to each other and produce sedation as a side effect. Because of this, they are called *narcotics* (producing sleep or narcosis). Morphine, one of our oldest and most effective drugs, is most familiar. Codeine is a mild narcotic. A number of other drugs, modified in chemical laboratories, are classed as narcotics, as, of course, is heroin, which presently has no legitimate medical use in this country. Besides relief of pain, narcotics may be prescribed to control severe cough and diarrhea; in general, they depress the breathing centers and have a constipating effect.

The great hazard of narcotics is that they are addictive if taken over a prolonged time. Addiction has two main features: development of tolerance, and a withdrawal syndrome. "Tolerance" means that one needs a greater and greater dose to do the same job. On stopping an addictive drug, the body may react with an illness known as withdrawal syndrome, caused by lack of the accustomed drug. A withdrawal syndrome is an illness that develops on stopping an addictive drug. Narcotics addicts, alcohol addicts, and perhaps even exercise addicts develop withdrawal symptoms on stopping their "habit." Surprisingly, the most dangerous withdrawal syndrome is that of alcohol cessation.

All other pain relievers are grouped as "non-narcotic analgesics." Of these, probably none is remarkably better than aspirin, which is not a totally innocuous drug. Aspirin and other salicylates can cause bleeding and erosion of the stomach lining. Toxic effects of large doses include mild to severe symptoms such as stomach distress, ringing in the ears, and nausea; acute salicylate poisoning is a medical emergency. In ordinary occasional low dosage, bad reactions are quite rare, but small bleeding points in the stomach lining may occur without being recognized. *Phenacetin* and *acetaminophen* have about the same pain-relieving and fever-reducing actions as aspirin, but without aspirin's anti-inflammatory properties.

A few drugs fit in neither camp. *Pentazocine* is a derivative of the narcotic family, but seems less addictive and has been licensed as a non-narcotic.

Aspirin and other non-narcotic analgesics are often combined in over-the-counter mixtures. There seems to be only slight value in these combinations over plain aspirin. APC combinations (aspirin, phenacetin, and caffeine) are sold under many trade names. Sometimes they are combined with codeine, in which case they are designated as "compound."

Anti-inflammatory agents

Inflammation is a response by the body to infection, injury, tumors, and causes unknown. The body shunts fluid and cells into a local area. The resulting swelling is usually red, warm, and painful.

The cause of inflammation should be found and treated, but this is not always possible. Arthritic and rheumatic diseases that cause joint inflammation are the best examples of disorders of unknown cause treated with anti-inflammatory agents.

Aspirin is an anti-inflammatory agent, as are *indomethacin, phenylbutazone,* and *ibuprofen.* A common side effect of these drugs is gastrointestinal irritation.

Another group of anti-inflammatory agents is the *corticosteroids,* sometimes simply called "steroids," which are derived from or closely related to cortisone. Most of them have "-sone" or "-one" in their names; for example, *hydrocortisone, prednisone, prednisolone, methylprednisolone, triamcinolone,* and other brand names too numerous to mention.

These are powerful drugs. A "shot" may quiet an exquisitely painful joint in a day or two, or treatment, as with the first cortisone preparations, may enable a bedridden arthritic patient to get up and walk. But along with a great capacity for doing good, they have a malevolent propensity for causing numerous side effects on prolonged administration.

Adverse reactions. The corticosteroids may decrease resistance to infection and mask symptoms; may provoke peptic ulcer and diabetes, bone softening (osteoporosis), and acne; and may cause cataracts. The drugs also may cause water retention, weight gain, and redistribution of fat. Mild to severe mental reactions may range from depression to euphoria.

The full catalog of side effects is much longer, but would only emphasize the necessity of medical judgment in determining when and if to initiate steroid treatment, the smallest effective dose, when to taper off or withdraw, and watchfulness for adverse reactions that may disappear or be minimized by regulation of therapy.

Cough remedies

A cough is a defensive mechanism that ejects foreign matter from the respiratory system. A cough serves a purpose when it is "productive"—that is, it may cough out stagnant material when there is infection in the breathing passages. But a cough also may be dry, unproductive, painful, and a nagging nuisance that keeps one awake at night.

There is no shortage of cough remedies offered to the public—frequently, on TV, by a soothing spouse who dispenses a capsule or liquid to a cruelly suffering mate who is beatific over all the attention. Cough medicines are traditionally of two sorts: suppressants or expectorants. Many remedies contain both, although the actions are theoretically antagonistic.

Cough suppressants are all narcotics or narcotic derivatives. Codeine is most often used, but all narcotics will suppress a cough. In low dosage, they may be obtained without a prescription; but in higher dosage, they must be prescribed by a physician who is licensed to prescribe narcotics. When given to relieve pain after a surgical operation, narcotics suppress coughing and may lead to collections of mucus in the lungs—and possibly even to post-operative pneumonia.

Expectorants do not suppress a cough but tend to liquefy the sputum and make it easier to be coughed up. Expectorant drugs in many cough remedies include *acetylcysteine, glyceryl guaiacolate,* and *potassium iodide.* Probably the simplest, cheapest, and most effective expectorant of all is inhaled water vapor. The old-fashioned "croup tent," a canopy wherein one inhales warm water vapor from a heated container, is excellent, but a steam kettle, vaporizer, or nebulizer also serves well. Patients who have bronchitis often feel better and cough more easily after a hot shower. Needless to say, it is not the play of water on the skin but the steamy atmosphere that has helped.

Does it make sense to combine expectorants and cough suppressants in the same medication? Probably not. Generally, the most harmless treatment for a cough is an expectorant, of which water vapor is the best. Then a cough suppressant can sometimes be added in the evening when the cough interferes with sleep. However, the use of any cough suppressant is hazardous in a person who smokes or is a devotee of alcohol or other sedative drugs. Such drugs depress the body's mechanism for cleaning the bronchi (breathing tubes) and make a cough even more important to avoid serious lung infection.

Vitamins

Vitamins are very tiny amounts of chemical substances provided by foods. Many vitamins act as parts of enzymes, which are protein molecules that we synthesize from foods. It may seem questionable to include vitamins in a discussion of drugs and medicines, except that innumerable people apparently think of them as super-drugs that act like an all-purpose tonic to keep one aburst with health.

Lack of vitamins does cause deficiency diseases such as scurvy, rickets, and beriberi, but such disorders are rare in the United States. Most physicians seldom prescribe vitamins. The greatest use of vitamins is not medical but personal, by people who take them as insurance of good health, or better-than-good health. Most normal diets furnish more than the required daily amounts of vitamins. The marvelous adaptive chemistry of the body can make at least one preformed vitamin, niacin, quite unnecessary in the diet. The body can synthesize it from tryptophan, an amino acid that is plentiful in most proteins.

The main distinction of so-called "natural" vitamins is that they are expensive and supposedly more magical because of their exotic source. All vitamins are natural in that nature has decreed a specific molecular structure for each of them; otherwise, it isn't a vitamin. The molecule is the same whether it is synthesized in a laboratory or present in seaweed, and it makes not a whit of difference to the body.

The accompanying table lists the fundamental functions and actions of vitamins as presently understood by medical science.

Laxatives

Healthy people have as many as three or four bowel movements a day, and as few as one or two a week. The frequency and bulk of the stool depend mainly on the amount of undigestible material eaten. As one gets

Vitamins and their functions

Vitamin	Usual source	Deficiency disease	Usual associated state leading to this disease	Danger of overdosage	Comments
A	eggs, milk, meat, vegetables	night blindness, corneal ulcers	bowel diseases with malabsorption (sprue, cystic fibrosis, and others)	weight loss, itching, abdominal and joint pain	Eating polar bear liver, rich in this vitamin, can cause serious illness.
B_1 = thiamine	plants	beriberi, Wernicke-Korsakoff syndrome	alcoholism, intestinal diseases with malabsorption	none	A diet of white rice (alone) can cause this disorder. Simply including the rice hulls prevents the beriberi.
B_2 = riboflavin	milk, eggs, liver, meat	skin rash	pellagra	none	
B_6 = pyridoxine	plants	neuritis when INH is taken	tuberculosis	none	Given along with certain drugs that cause nerve damage.
Unnumbered B Groups					
Pantothenic acid	plants	none known	none	none	There is no clear use in humans.
Niacin and nicotinic acid	made from tryptophan	pellagra	alcoholism or pure corn diet	flushing, liver damage	Part of protein malnutrition.
Folic acid	plants	anemia	alcoholism	none	

Vitamin	Usual source	Deficiency disease	Usual associated state leading to this disease	Danger of overdosage	Comments
B$_{12}$	meats	anemia, neurologic disease	none	none	Not a "tonic"; actually, only useful to treat pernicious anemia.
C = ascorbic acid	plants (especially fruits)	scurvy (the first deficiency disease recognized . . . in 1757)	long sea voyages without fresh food	diarrhea, urine acidosis (dangerous in a patient with gout)	Popularly thought to prevent or "cure" colds. So far, studies are contradictory.
D	sunlight needed for conversion of Vitamin D in humans	rickets	none	hypercalcemia, diarrhea, kidney damage, high blood pressure	There is a narrow range between therapeutic and damaging dosages.
E	plants, oils	anemia in premature infants	prematurity	increased sensitivity to the cardiac drug, digitalis	Popular belief that this vitamin helps sexual function in humans is unwarranted.
K	plants, bacteria, meats	bleeding, usually only when on drugs to counteract vitamin K	anticoagulant therapy, liver disease	none	It seems impossible to find a diet deficient in vitamin K. However, there are uses in some blood-clotting disorders.

older, the bowels often become a bit more sluggish. Also, many diseases of maturity, such as diabetes, affect bowel function. Probably the most common cause of poor bowel function—usually complained of as constipation—is the overuse of laxatives. More and more, the tendency is to urge people to discontinue all laxatives that act by irritating the bowel or drawing water into the stool, and instead just to eat a quantity of dietary fiber.

Anticoagulants

We expect a scratch or small wound to stop bleeding quite soon and to start to heal itself. Coagulation of blood seals holes in vessels and prevents continuous bleeding, and is accomplished by a complex system of clotting factors (elements) in the blood. Occasionally this system is overactive, leading to abnormal clotting and disease.

Thrombophlebitis is a disorder in which clots form within veins, usually in the leg. Worse yet, bits of clot may break off and float through the bloodstream to the lungs where they cause more damage, even fatalities. Clots also may form within the heart, especially in the presence of arrhythmias or a narrowed mitral valve. In these disorders, it seems clear that treatment with drugs that decrease clotting is beneficial.

Many other disorders involving disease of blood vessels have been treated with anticoagulants. Coronary artery disease causing angina pectoris—heart pain on exertion—or myocardial infarction, a "heart attack," have been treated with these drugs. Strokes and transient ischemic attacks of cerebral-vascular disease have been similarly treated. Unfortunately, there is conflicting evidence as to the value of anticoagulants in such diseases, and their use requires clinical judgment.

Two main groups of anticoagulants now available are *heparin* and *coumarin,* which act against clotting elements in the blood.

Aspirin, *sulfinpyrazone (Arturane), dipyridamole (Persantine),* and other drugs act against the blood platelet, a cell fragment that seems to initiate some clotting.

Heparin is a large molecule found in many animal tissues. It can be administered only by injection, and is usually given intravenously for several days to several weeks, obviously in a hospital. Heparin works immediately, by obstructing the function of clotting factors already formed in the blood.

Warfarins, which include *coumadin* and *panwarfarin,* interfere with the liver's use of vitamin K in synthesizing clotting factors. Because of this, the action of warfarin is delayed for several days (until previously synthesized clotting factors are used up). The most common treatment program is to give heparin intravenously for several days, and warfarin orally. Then when tests indicate that the warfarin is taking effect, the heparin can be stopped.

The value of interfering with platelet function is still unclear, and the use of drugs that have such action is somewhat experimental. It may well be that in the future the use of such drugs will be extensive.

Adverse effects. Since coagulation protects against unwanted bleeding, the major hazard of anticoagulant therapy is excessive "thinning" of the blood so that it leaks out abnormally. Patients may bleed into the urine, bowels, internal spaces, lungs, and skin, and such bleeding is more likely following accidents or injuries. Patients on these drugs should wear bracelets or identifying devices stating that they are taking anticoagulants. When taking anticoagulants, bleeding can be more serious than the condition for which the drugs were given.

Warfarin dosage varies considerably from person to person, and is strikingly affected by many other drugs, including the ubiquitous aspirin. Patients on warfarin are usually told to avoid any drugs not cleared by their physician. A blood test called the Quick prothrombin test-time (P.T.)—named for its inventor, Dr. Quick—is used to monitor the dosage. Prothrombin is one of the natural clotting factors. The test is indeed quick, usually giving an answer in a few seconds. It measures the anti-clotting effect of warfarin so dosage can be kept at a desired level.

Patients on warfarin are advised to have their prothrombin times tested at least once a month, and in event of bleeding, to discontinue the medication and call their physician.

Hormones

Hormones are substances produced by the endocrine glands and fed into the bloodstream to send chemical messages to organs and tissues. When prescribed as drugs, they are given either to replace or supplement natural secretions, or, in larger dosages, because of some unphysiologic action. The hormones most often prescribed are either natural agents, or related chemicals synthetically produced, which parallel the secretions of the thyroid, pancreas, ovary, testis, or adrenal gland. Other organs, notably the pituitary gland, also produce hormones, but their secretions are seldom used therapeutically.

Thyroid hormones include the drugs *triiodothyronine* or T_3, *thyroxine* or T_4, combinations, and other compounds. All have similar action, which, broadly speaking, is to fan body fires to burn more intensely—in effect, to step up energies. Probably the most "natural" agent paralleling normal thyroid secretion is thyroxine. Its major use is to replace deficient thyroid secretion.

Thyroid hormones are not harmless pills to give energy. In excess, they lead to hyperthyroidism or thyrotoxicosis, with serious effects—weakness, restlessness, swings of emotion, tremor, sweating, appetite upsets, and heart irritation. They burn the candle at both ends, which gives a lovely light but soon exhausts the candle. Use of large doses of thyroid hormone as "reducing pills"—which can indeed cause weight loss—is quite hazardous, since the desired effect is attained only by developing a serious disease, hyperthyroidism.

Insulin and glucagon. These hormones are produced by the pancreas gland.

The adrenal gland produces *aldosterone* and *cortisol*. Either or both may be lacking, as in Addison's disease, and can be replaced by synthetic drugs with closely related and variously modified actions.

However, these agents have remarkable anti-inflammatory effects when used in appropriate dosage, and their major use is not simple replacement therapy.

Secretions of the adrenal gland, and others, are controlled by the "master gland," the pituitary. The pituitary hormone, which stimulates the adrenals, is adrenocorticotropic hormone (ACTH). It can be given by injection to cause the adrenal gland to produce large amounts of cortisol. However, the same effect can be achieved by giving inexpensive oral doses of synthetic cortisol-like drugs so there is little therapeutic need for ACTH.

The ovaries and testes produce eggs and sperm, as well as hormones of some popularity. The ovaries produce estrogens, probably better known as "female hormones." The testes produce androgens such as testosterone.

The sex hormones, adrenal cortex hormones, and in fact cholesterol, share a common molecular nucleus and are collectively classed as *steroids*. Certain chemical modifications of male hormones are the so-called "anabolic steroids," which are intended to be low in sex effects but high in their "building up" effects on muscles and tissues. They are sometimes used by athletes who hope to become huskier and more combative than they are. The use of these drugs for such purpose is medically, if not athletically, discredited.

Hundreds of drugs are available, many under dozens of trade names and in dozens of combinations. Textbooks of pharmacology run to more than 1,000 pages and require sophisticated knowledge of chemistry and physiology. Lacking such special knowledge, what can an intelligent person do? The following rules may provide some general guidelines:

● All drugs are potentially dangerous, whether sold by prescription or over the counter.

● All drugs have the potential for serious adverse side effects.

● Drugs are to be used for specific purposes, not as an all-purpose health tonic.

● The more drugs you take at one time, the more complex the interactions and the more likely you are to have an unexpected bad result.

● Every patient should know the names of the drugs he takes, their actions, and possible bad effects. He should discuss this with his physician and be sure he understands directions for use.

● Often no medication at all is the best prescription. If the hazard of the drug is greater than the hazard of the illness, the drug should not be given.

● Medicines work best when taken exactly as prescribed. Don't double or halve the dose, omit the drug, or change the frequency.